The Picture Life of
★ GEORGE BUSH ★

The Picture Life of

GEORGE
★ BUSH ★

by Ron Schneiderman

Franklin Watts   1989
New York   London   Toronto   Sydney

Cover photo courtesy of Gamma-Liaison (Cynthia Johnson)

Photographs courtesy of: AP/Wide World Photos: pp. 6, 9, 11, 12, 39,
49, 60; The White House: pp. 15, 51 (bottom), 54 ; © Paul Seligman
1989: p. 20; UPI/Bettmann Newsphotos: pp. 24, 25, 28, 44, 47, 51
(top), 53, 57; John Burns/Life: p. 33; Central Intelligence Agency:
p. 34; Liaison Agency/Cynthia Johnson: pp. 41, 59 (top right); Liaison
Agency/Diana Walker: p. 59 (top left and bottom).

Library of Congress Cataloging-in-Publication Data

Schneiderman, Ron.

The picture life of George Bush/by Ron Schneiderman.
p. cm.
Includes index.
Summary: Traces the life and accomplishments of the war hero,
millionaire businessman, congressman, CIA director, and president of
the United States.
ISBN 0-531-10696-9
1. Bush, George, 1924– — Pictorial works. 2. Presidents — United
States — Biography — Pictorial works. [1. Bush, George, 1924–   .
2. Presidents.] I. Title.
E882.S36   1989
973.927′092′4 — dc19
[B]   [92]   88-34543   CIP   AC

★ Contents ★

Chapter One
Coming of Age 7

Chapter Two
Washington Calls 18

Chapter Three
Serving Two Presidents 26

Chapter Four
A Presidential Contender 36

Chapter Five
Vice President Bush 46

Chapter Six
President Bush 56

Index 63

★ One ★
COMING
OF AGE

George Herbert Walker Bush was one of five children. His parents, Dorothy Walker and Prescott Sheldon Bush, had met and married soon after Prescott returned from Army service in World War I.

George's brother, Pres, Jr., was born in 1922, while his parents lived in St. Louis. By the time George was born on June 12, 1924, the family had moved to Milton, Massachusetts, where his father had taken a job with U.S. Rubber Co. Eventually, they moved to Greenwich, Connecticut, to be closer to the company's headquarters in New York City.

*Six-year-old George and
his sister Nancy in 1930*

A Republican, George's father was very interested in politics and became active in state party activities. In 1950, at the age of fifty-five, Prescott Bush ran for his first political office, United States Senator, against Senator William Benton. He lost, but made a good showing. When the state's senior senator died two years later, George's father was nominated to run in a special election to fill the time remaining on Senator Benton's term of office. He won and was re-elected in 1956.

He retired from the U.S. Senate in 1962, becoming a managing partner in an investment banking company. George's father died at age 72. His mother, Dorothy Walker Bush, now 87 years old, still lives at Walker's Point, the family's waterfront retreat in Kennebunkport, Maine. George's mother was born in Kennebunkport and his parents were married in the town. His grandfather, George Herbert Walker, a New York stockbroker, and Walker's father, David, had purchased the property in 1903. The eleven-acre estate has a three-story, twenty-six-room house with nine bedrooms, a smaller home for George's mother, and several other cottages. The property is about two miles up a private road. From the age of four, George spent part of every summer there, except during World War II when he was in the Navy.

The Bush children, George's older brother Pres, his younger brothers Bucky and Jonathan, and his sister Nancy, liked to play games. Dorothy Bush, a one-time national women's tennis finalist, taught them to be competitive, but always to be team players, who, even if they were the stars of the game, would give other players credit. Poor sportsmanship was never allowed. Bush children who protested a decision made in favor of another brother or sister were sent to their rooms.

Outdoor sports were always stressed in the Bush household. In 1939, George (left) was one of the finalists in a field club junior tennis tournament.

There were always plenty of friends around. During the day, the children sailed and played tennis; at night they played board games. George was the most competitive of all the children, but he was always fair. And he was always willing to share, so much so that some of his friends started calling him "Have-Half."

That nickname didn't last very long since everyone in the family called George either "Little Pop" or "Poppy" (his grandfather was called "Pop"). Eventually, it was just "Poppy." They continued to call him that until he left home to join the Navy.

George never really thought of his family as being wealthy, but he was driven to Greenwich Country Day School by a chauffeur, and there were other servants in the house. He attended Phillips Academy, a private prep school in Andover, Massachusetts. Most of the students were from wealthy families.

By the time George had graduated from Phillips, World War II was well under way. Secretary of War Henry Stimson delivered the commencement address at George's graduation. In his speech, Stimson said the war would be a long one, and even though America needed fighting men, George and his classmates would better serve the country by continuing their education before getting into uniform.

As a child, George Bush attended private schools. This picture is from the 1942 Phillips Academy yearbook, not long before Bush (1st row center) joined the Navy.

George wasn't convinced. He had already told his father that college would have to wait—he was planning to join the Navy and hoped to become a naval aviator. In June 1942, on his eighteenth birthday, just after graduating from Phillips, George enlisted in the U.S. Navy Reserve as a Seaman Second Class.

Because his grades were good, especially in mathematics, he qualified for pilot training. Pilots were in short supply, so the Navy had trimmed its aviator-training program to ten months. George won his wings and became an officer in the U.S. Navy while he was still eighteen, making him the youngest pilot in the Navy at the time.

George Bush just after he received his commission as an officer in the U.S. Navy.

He shipped out to the South Pacific on the aircraft carrier *San Jacinto*. His gunner, Leo Nadeau, had painted "Barbara" in big white letters under the cockpit of his Grumman Avenger bomber. Bush had met Barbara Pierce, the daughter of the publisher of *McCall's* magazine, during a prep-school Christmas dance. They became secretly engaged during the summer of 1943, but finally told their families and friends later that year—just before George was assigned to a bomber squadron that was training for duty in the Pacific.

George Goes to War • It wasn't long before George was seeing action. On September 2, 1944, he was flying his torpedo-equipped bomber in a formation of several other aircraft during an invasion of one of the South Pacific islands being held by the Japanese. Jack Delaney was his tail gunner and radio operator. William G. White, another gunner, was filling in for Leo Nadeau. The target that day was a Japanese communications center.

Bush put his plane into a dive, but he suddenly felt the aircraft lurch. He knew he had been hit. Within seconds, his cockpit filled with smoke. Close calls weren't a new experience to Bush; he had already survived several, including a forced landing in the ocean when his fuel tank sprang a leak.

Even though his plane was on fire, Bush continued to dive at his target, dropping four 500-pound bombs before turning his Grumman Avenger toward the sea. Somehow, he managed to level off and told Delaney and White to bail out. Then Bush parachuted from the burning plane, which moments later crashed into the sea. He couldn't see Delaney and White. As he swam to his tiny raft, Bush worried about the Japanese boats he had spotted leaving the island, apparently in an effort to pick him up. But several American fighter pilots saw them, too, and drove them back to the island with gunfire. Bush drifted for hours before he was picked up by an American submarine, the U.S.S. *Finback*.

Bush didn't learn until he got aboard the sub that Delaney and White didn't make it. One went down with the plane; the other jumped, but his parachute didn't open.

For completing his mission, even after his plane was on fire, Bush was awarded the Distinguished Flying Cross. Once he got back to shore, Bush spent several months resting and recuperating before returning to combat duty. He eventually flew a total of 1,228 hours as a Navy pilot, and was awarded three Air Medals.

Back to School • George and Barbara were married just two weeks after he returned from the war. She

George and Barbara on their wedding day in 1945

had completed two years at Smith College, but dropped out to be with George, who was just entering Yale University. Like his father before him, he became a member of Skull and Bones, the top social club at Yale. It wasn't long before he became a "Big Man on Campus," a role he didn't particularly like. When it came time for his pledge class at the club to elect its president, George was immediately nominated. But he said he didn't want the job. "I don't think I'm the right guy," he said. He was elected anyway.

Always a natural athlete, Bush also joined the Yale baseball team. He was good with the glove and a fair hitter, but not very fast. As a junior, he hit .239, good enough to help Yale get into the National Collegiate Athletic Association finals, but not good enough to win; Yale lost in the final to the University of California. The following year, he became captain of the team and hit .264. This time, Yale lost the championship to Southern California, two games to one. Bush only got two hits in twelve times at bat during the championship series, but he scored Yale's only run in the opening game, and knocked in two runs with a single in the team's 8–3 win in the second game. Bush graduated from Yale with a degree in economics. He was named a member of Phi Beta Kappa, the national honor society for U.S. college students and graduates with top grades.

The Bushes Move to Texas • After George's graduation, the Bushes moved to Midland, Texas. A family friend, Neil Mallon, had offered Bush a job as a trainee for Dresser Industries, a large oil company. He worked as a salesman for Dresser in west Texas and California from 1948 to 1950. But Bush was ambitious. After two years, he and a neighbor set up a company that would purchase royalty rights from small landowners, which means they paid people for the right to drill for oil on their land.

Two years later, in 1953, he co-founded another company, Zapata Petroleum Corporation, to locate and buy oil-producing land, and a year later—at age thirty—he became president and co-founder of a third company, Zapata Offshore, which developed special platforms to drill for oil out in the ocean. Bush's uncle, Herbert Walker, was a big help in the future president's early business life, raising eight hundred thousand dollars through Eastern investors to help get the oil companies started. Today, much of the oil produced around the world is drilled with rigs developed by Zapata.

★ Two ★
WASHINGTON
CALLS

Bush found his life as a successful businessman very exciting and rewarding. From his beginnings as an equipment clerk, he had started his own company and was beginning to make a name for himself in the oil business—one of the most important industries in Texas.

But that happiness began to unravel in March 1953 when the Bushes' first daughter, Robin, who was born in Compton, California, in 1949, was diagnosed as having leukemia, a form of cancer. The doctors told her parents that there really wasn't anything they could do for her; they said she didn't have very long to live—weeks, maybe months.

Stunned by the news, Bush called his uncle, Dr. John Walker, in New York City, seeking advice. Dr.

Walker was a cancer specialist and president of New York's Memorial Hospital. He suggested that the Bushes bring Robin to New York for treatment.

Over the next six months, Robin's health actually improved at times. In fact, there were periods when she looked perfectly healthy and acted like any other child her age. But she was still very sick. While Barbara stayed with her, Bush spent six very difficult months traveling between his business in Texas and New York. Despite the best care they could give her, Robin died just a few months before her fourth birthday. Like all parents who have lost a child, George and Barbara took Robin's death very hard and still find it hard to accept.

A Need for More Recognition • By the early 1960s, Bush was the father of five—four boys, "little" George, Jeb, Neil, Marvin; and a girl, Dorothy—and he was a millionaire. Living in Houston, he began to feel that his business success wasn't enough. He felt he needed more personal recognition. He also wanted to become an even bigger part of the community, as his father had been. Also, having done well in business, he was now less concerned about the family's financial security and paying for his children's education. Politics was an obvious outlet. He became active in local Republican party activities, and in

George and Barbara Bush at home in Texas in 1964 with their children, Neil, Dorothy, Marvin, and Jeb (missing is their eldest son, George, Jr.)

Bush campaigns for the Senate from Texas, in September 1964. Although Bush won the Republican primary race, he lost to Democrat Ralph Yarborough in the general election.

1962, he was named chairman of the Harris County Republican organization.

It was the beginning of a political career that probably went beyond his wildest dreams.

A Run for Congress • People around Houston were beginning to notice Bush's efforts and he wanted a bigger role in the Texas Republican party. So, in 1964, just two years after taking on the Harris County party position, Bush decided to run for elective office. Even though he still wasn't known very well throughout the state, he ran for the U.S. Senate. Bush campaigned hard, and won the preliminary Republican primary race against three other candidates with 44 percent of the vote. He beat more widely known Republican candidates in the runoff election to decide who would face Senator Ralph Yarborough, a Democrat, in the general election. But he didn't have a chance against Yarborough, even though he ran a hard campaign. Lyndon B. Johnson, a popular, life-long Texan, was the Democratic candidate for president and swept the state in the general election, which helped Yarborough. Bush lost to Senator Yarborough by 330,000 votes.

By 1966, Bush had lowered his sights somewhat. In February, just fifteen months after his unsuccessful run for the U.S. Senate, he resigned as chairman and chief executive officer of Zapata to run full-time for a newly created seat in the U.S. House of Representatives from a Houston suburb. Much better known in west Texas by now, Bush was taken more seriously. He won easily with 57.1 percent of the vote.

The Bushes Move to Washington • Once he got to Washington, Bush got right into the swing of things. Even though he was a freshman congressman, he was named to the House Ways and Means Committee, which advised Congress on financial matters, including tax legislation, and controlled committee appointments. His support and vote also helped create the Environmental Protection Agency to protect the nation's air, water, and other natural resources from pollution.

A Run for the Senate • In 1970, Bush considered running for the U.S. Senate again. It was a tough decision. He had already been re-elected to the House once and was confident he could be re-elected after having served two terms.

Bush knew it was risky, but he finally decided to take the plunge. Everyone knew it was going to be a close race. Bush ran a strong campaign. But even though he got more than a million votes, Bush lost the election with 46 percent of the vote.

As bad as he felt about the defeat during his last few weeks in Congress, Bush at least knew he had something to fall back on—if he wanted it. President Nixon had promised him a job if he lost the Senate race. There was no discussion about a particular job, but Bush let it be known to senior members of the White House staff that he was very interested in foreign affairs. In fact, he began to tell aides closest to the president that he wanted to be Ambassador to the United Nations. Nixon appointed him to the job in 1971. The Senate approved him, even though several senators complained that he lacked foreign policy experience.

As World War II was drawing to a close in 1945, the UN was organized to deal with quarrels that might lead to future wars between nations. Today, this worldwide organization remains a place where nations can discuss—even argue—their views in the interest of world peace. It also helps nations protect the rights of their people, feed their poor, and even build much needed facilities, such as dams.

Bush's biggest effort while at the UN was to try to keep Taiwan in the world organization, along with the People's Republic of China (PRC), sometimes known as Mainland China or Red China. President Nixon wanted both Chinese nations, but this conflicted with a 1964 campaign position Bush had taken

In 1970, President Richard Nixon appointed Bush
to the post of Ambassador to the United Nations.

*U.S. Ambassador George Bush uses his glasses
—for biting, holding, and peering over,
but not for looking through—as he listens
during a UN session in 1971.*

that called for the United States to leave the UN if the PRC were admitted to the world body.

The United States Is Outvoted • But the United States was outvoted; the PRC was admitted to the UN while Taiwan was pushed out. Although Bush wasn't blamed for the defeat, his stay at the UN was short. He served as U.S. ambassador to the United Nations until January 1973, when President Nixon had another job for him.

★ Three ★
SERVING TWO PRESIDENTS

Bush was called back to Washington. President Nixon asked him to come out to Camp David, the presidential retreat in the nearby hills of Maryland, for a talk. But before he boarded the helicopter for the trip from the Pentagon, Bush was asked to meet with George Shultz, who was then secretary of the treasury. This was Nixon's second term as president and Bush had heard that several important changes were in the works. New people were being brought in to help the president. For one thing, Nixon was planning to put together a "super cabinet" headed by his top advisors. They would work closely with the president and they would appoint strong deputies to actually run their departments.

That's just what Shultz had in mind when he asked to meet with Bush. Shultz told Bush he wanted him to be his deputy secretary of the treasury. It sounded interesting, but Bush said that he had to talk to the president later that day before he could even consider the offer.

Another New Post • Of course, Nixon knew that Bush had talked to Shultz and why. He told Bush that if he really wanted the treasury job, he should take it. But the president had something different in mind for him.

Nixon told Bush that he wanted him to run the Republican National Committee, the party's national organization. He impressed upon Bush that it was a critical time for the party and that he expected a lot of changes in the coming years. He thought Bush could be an important part of that. As chairman of the Republican National Committee, Bush would be replacing Senator Robert Dole of Kansas, whom he would later face in the race for the 1988 presidential nomination. Dole was not a favorite with the Nixon White House. He was considered to be too independent and outspoken. Bush, on the other hand, was "loyal" and "a party man," someone who could be trusted and counted on to support President Nixon.

*Bush, President Nixon's choice to head
the Republican National Committee, is
shown here in 1973 with his predecessor,
Robert Dole (left) of Kansas.*

Bush took the job and quickly demonstrated that he was a party man, but not a servant of the Nixon Administration. He worked closely with state Republican party organizations. In his first year as national party chairman, he flew all over the country, giving over one hundred speeches and holding almost as many press conferences.

Bush's most difficult problem, however, was trying to defend President Nixon and his aides in the Watergate scandal.

Watergate is the name of an office and apartment building in Washington, D.C. Late in the night on June 17, 1972, seven men—including a former FBI agent, a former CIA agent, a security specialist for the Committee to Re-elect the President, and four Cuban-Americans—broke into the office of the Democratic National Headquarters offices in the Watergate building to steal important papers and plant electronic listening devices. They were caught by a Watergate security guard. White House aides, afraid that the publicity from the burglary attempt would hurt Nixon's chances of re-election, tried to cover up the story.

The official Republican National Committee, which Bush headed, had nothing to do with the scandal. However, since he represented the president's political party, Bush was in the uncomfortable position of having to defend the president and his aides.

But the scandal got bigger and bigger, and despite efforts by Nixon's top aides to keep information about the burglary and the cover-up from leaking out, stories appeared on the front pages of every newspaper in the country (and many foreign ones) every day for months. It was becoming clear that several top White House staff members were involved.

President Nixon was under a great deal of pressure—from the press, the public, and most members of Congress—to resign. Bush realized that as head of the national Republican party organization, he had to act. On August 7, 1974, he wrote a letter to Nixon in which he strongly suggested that the president resign. The letter said the resignation would be best for the country and best for the president. It was delivered the day after what turned out to be President Nixon's last cabinet meeting. Nixon resigned the presidency three days later.

The Ford Years • When Gerald R. Ford succeeded Nixon as president, Bush was mentioned as his possible vice president. He wanted the job. In fact, Bush more or less asked for the job by letting key Ford associates and aides know that he very much wanted to be vice president. But it wasn't to be. President

Ford called Bush at his home in Maine and informed him that he had selected New York Governor Nelson A. Rockefeller for the post.

Obviously disappointed, Bush asked to see the president. He told Ford that he was resigning as chairman of the national committee. Apparently prepared for this, Ford mentioned that two very important diplomatic posts were about to open up—Ambassador to Great Britain and Ambassador to France. Either position would have given Bush a great deal of influence in the nation's relationship with a major European ally. But Bush knew David Bruce was about to leave his post as chief of the United States liaison office in Beijing (then called Peking), the capital of the People's Republic of China. He told Ford that's the job he really wanted. President Ford was surprised, but Bush thought the Far East would be more of a challenge—and more of an adventure—than Europe. In fact, he had already discussed it with Barbara; if George was offered an overseas post of his choice, they decided they wanted to go to China. He got the job.

The Bushes were busy as soon as they were settled in China. They met regularly, both on official business and socially, with members of the Chinese government and with other diplomats stationed in Beijing. Even though they were provided with an official car in China, the Bushes decided they would be a little different. They began riding bicycles just about everywhere they went, just like the Chinese, who called them the "Bushers."

Meeting Mao • During the sixteen months he lived in China, Bush met only once with the country's fabled leader, Mao Tse-tung, when Secretary of State Henry Kissinger arrived to discuss President Ford's official visit to China later in the year.

It wasn't very long before the Bushes were packing their bags again. Bush had received an urgent message from Kissinger in late 1975; the president wanted Bush to consent to be nominated as director of the Central Intelligence Agency.

It was a tough decision. The Bushes liked living in China. Also, Bush was concerned that if he took the CIA job, the Chinese people—at least the country's leaders—would think that he had been a spy all the time he was in China. Bush also wanted to stay close to politics and he worried that he was being pushed into a nonpolitical position. Still, he found it difficult to say no to the president of the United States.

At the CIA • As it turned out, Bush's move to the CIA was part of a major administration shake-up at the end of October. Several key Ford aides had sud-

The bicycling Bushes became a common sight in Beijing during the years Bush served in China. Because the United States did not have formal diplomatic relations with China at the time, Bush wasn't actually ambassador, but as chief of the U.S. liaison mission, he was the highest ranking United States official there.

In 1975, President Ford appointed Bush to head the Central Intelligence Agency. In keeping with the agency's secrecy, little is known of Bush's activities during this period.

denly lost their jobs, including CIA Director William Colby, who had been an American intelligence officer since World War II.

When Bush arrived at the CIA it was under congressional investigation for illegal domestic spying and other serious charges of wrongdoing. Under the law, the CIA is only allowed to operate outside the

United States. To the surprise of many, including top CIA professionals, Bush managed to bring some order to the agency and restored much of its confidence. He named a new deputy director, someone who was respected within the agency, and moved several top CIA people into new jobs. Some were promoted. Others retired, resigned, or were discharged.

Briefing President-Elect Carter • Probably the least enjoyable part of his job as CIA director came when Jimmy Carter, the former governor of Georgia, defeated President Ford in the presidential election of 1976. During the campaign, Carter had made a much-publicized speech in which he said that Presidents Nixon and Ford had used government positions as "dumping grounds" for unsuccessful candidates for political office—and he specifically mentioned Bush as an example, namely his UN appointment in 1971.

But as CIA director, Bush was required to regularly inform the new president-elect about activities in foreign countries. On his last visit with Carter at his home in Plains, Georgia, in November 1976, Bush told Carter that he was resigning so that Carter could name his own CIA chief.

★ Four ★
A PRESIDENTIAL CONTENDER

Bush now found himself with a lot of time on his hands. He didn't have a job. Independently wealthy, he could afford to spend some time serving on several committees. One that met regularly was the Trilateral Commission, a group of well-known leaders from the United States, Europe, and Japan who were concerned about international affairs. But he also spent the next two years running for president.

Impressed with the way Jimmy Carter had gotten his name before the public and made known his views on important issues, Bush decided to take the same approach. He traveled from state to state, talking to large and small groups, meeting with state and local political leaders, hoping to win early primary elections. He was also getting more attention from the press.

During his campaign, he supported the expansion of nuclear power, although he called for the improvement of safety procedures at nuclear power plants. He proposed a $20 billion tax cut, about half of which would go to individuals to encourage them to save or invest in home purchases; the other half would go to the business community to invest and to hire and train young workers. He also expressed concern about the Soviet buildup of its military arms and called for the restoration of new weapons systems canceled by President Carter, including the B-1 bomber.

Bush began making some points, especially with women voters, when he supported the Equal Rights Amendment to the Constitution, which would require that all federal and state laws uphold the rights of men and women equally. California Governor Ronald Reagan, another presidential candidate, opposed the amendment.

The Race Begins • In November 1979, Bush narrowly beat Senator Howard H. Baker, Jr., of Tennessee in the Maine primary. Barely three months later, he beat Reagan, then the leading Republican candidate, in Iowa. Bush only topped Reagan by about 2,000 votes, but it was enough to move him ahead in the race for the Republican presidential nomination.

But the Iowa loss woke Reagan up. Dropping further behind Bush, according to a national survey, Reagan began to campaign harder in New Hampshire.

The Big Debate • The turning point in the important New Hampshire race came at what was supposed to be a two-man debate in Nashua between Bush and Reagan. The debate was jointly sponsored by the *Nashua Telegraph*, a local newspaper, and Reagan. Shortly before the debate was to begin, members of the Reagan staff decided to open the debate to other candidates—Senator Robert Dole, Senator Howard Baker, Congressman John Anderson of Illinois, and Phil Crane. Bush didn't like the idea. He only wanted to debate Reagan because, as he explained later, he believed that the audience was only interested in hearing the two of them.

The audience soon made it clear they wanted to hear all the candidates, but Jon Breen, the editor of the *Telegraph* and the debate moderator, said he wouldn't change his plans for the debate. And Bush refused to agree to an open forum. When Reagan began to explain to the audience why he felt the debate should include everyone, Breen ordered Rea-

Bush and Ronald Reagan (left) shake hands after a primary debate in Nashua, New Hampshire in 1980.

gan's microphone turned off. Reagan, getting angry, shouted, "I paid for this microphone." By that time, however, the other candidates had given up and left the stage.

The Bush-Reagan debate took place as originally planned, but the publicity hurt Bush politically. Many people thought he was unfair not to open the debate to the other candidates. Bush had made a mistake and he admitted it later. But it was too late. Reagan took 50 percent of the vote in the New Hampshire primary. Bush ran second, with 23 percent. The other four candidates shared the remaining votes.

The good news was that the campaign for a Republican candidate for president was quickly narrowing to a two-man contest; unfortunately for Bush, Reagan was gaining ground with each new primary race. Bush won some primary elections, but not as many as Reagan—and not the big ones.

One of his biggest setbacks came in March, in Illinois. Reagan was expected to win and he did. Bush hoped to finish at least a strong second, but he slipped to third place, behind John Anderson.

Some Help from TV • As the end of the primary season drew near, it looked as if Bush would get a break. Reagan had spent too much money on his campaign and had to cut back. Bush was able to spend more on TV and radio commercials and for travel. In April, Bush won the Pennsylvania primary and almost won in Texas, mainly as a result of a very effective paid TV program called "Ask George Bush," in which he responded to questions from an audience of friendly supporters.

But Reagan had built up too great a lead. Even though Bush beat Reagan in the important Michigan primary, tallies by major newspapers and TV networks reported that Reagan already had more than the 998 delegates needed to win the nomination at the Republican National Convention.

Bush campaigning in Dallas, Texas, in 1980

At that point, the race was more or less over. Besides Reagan's big delegate margin, Bush was now almost out of campaign money himself, and Reagan's big lead had significantly slowed Bush's ability to raise any more funds. As he explained later, Bush said he was taking the advice of a country and western song, "The Gambler," by Kenny Rogers, which was popular at the time: "You gotta know when to hold 'em, know when to fold 'em." Bush withdrew from the race for the presidential nomination on May 26.

At the Convention • The Republican convention was typical of huge political gatherings, full of excitement and rumors. It got off to a bang when former President Ford started talking publicly about the possibility of becoming Ronald Reagan's running mate. It would be the first time a former president ran for vice president.

The feeling among those at the convention was that a campaign with Reagan running for president and former President Ford as his running mate would be very strong against President Carter. But in TV interviews at the convention, Ford began describing how he thought he should operate as Reagan's vice president and what his responsibilities might be. It became clear that what Ford had in mind would give him more power than any previous vice president, and neither Reagan nor his supporters liked that idea. There could be only one president, one commander-in-chief, and they didn't want a former president in the White House working alongside a new president. The so-called Dream Ticket of Reagan and Ford fell through. When the two men met during the convention, they agreed it might be better if Ford simply helped Reagan in his campaign rather than run with him.

It didn't take Reagan long to make a decision. Within hours after his hastily called meeting with Ford, Reagan telephoned George Bush at his hotel and offered him the vice presidential spot on the ticket. Bush accepted, and shortly after midnight on July 17, Reagan ended all the guessing about his choice by going before the convention to announce that Bush would be his running mate.

As expected, the campaign was a busy one. Ronald Reagan and George Bush battled Jimmy Carter and his running mate, Walter Mondale, on just about every popular issue of the day, from maintaining a strong national defense, to social issues (such as how much support to give to the elderly), to giving special treatment to certain industries, like the oil companies. Bush was in favor of letting the oil companies set their own prices—an idea that was very popular in Texas and other oil-producing states, but not so pop-

ular with car owners, who worried that they might have to pay more for gas.

Reagan, meanwhile, was very effective in his criticism of President Carter's policies and actions, and also scored well in his only debate with Carter, which took place just six days before the election.

On November 4, Ronald Reagan and George Bush were elected in a landslide victory.

At the 1980 Republican Convention, George Bush was picked by Ronald Reagan to be his vice-presidential running mate. Shown from left to right: Bush, Reagan, Gerald Ford, and Nancy Reagan.

★ Five ★
VICE PRESIDENT BUSH

Despite the differences of the two men as candidates for the nomination, Bush quickly became one of Ronald Reagan's top supporters.

Bush kept busy. His vice presidency was full of the things that vice presidents usually do—he served as president of the U.S. Senate; held meetings with foreign dignitaries, both at home and abroad; and attended the funerals of several foreign heads of state as the representative of the United States. In fact, by his own count, from 1981 through the spring of 1987, he traveled to seventy-three foreign countries.

A Call from Washington • The relatively quiet pace of his duties was broken on March 30, 1981, during a trip to Texas to address a business group. *Air Force*

In his role as vice president, George Bush logged thousands of miles and visited many countries. He is shown here (top left) in 1985, visiting the El Obeid refugee camp in the Sudan, (top right) stopping at Grenada for nine hours on his way to Brazil, and, (left) in 1987, visiting the grounds of the former Nazi concentration camp of Auschwitz in Poland.

Two, the vice president's official plane, was racing down the runway, preparing for takeoff from Carswell Air Force Base, near Fort Worth, when the agent in charge of Bush's Secret Service detail told him that an urgent radio message had just come in from Washington: an attempt had been made on President Reagan's life.

Moments later, Bush got a call from Secretary of State Alexander Haig suggesting that he return to Washington immediately, rather than going on to Austin, Texas, as planned. Since the call was made to *Air Force Two* by radio, and the conversation could be picked up just about anywhere, Haig didn't offer very much information about what had actually happened. And he didn't say anything about the president's condition. Bush decided to wait for a coded message that was being sent to the plane's teletype machine. It wasn't until the message was decoded that Bush learned the president had been shot.

Air Force Two stopped in Austin only long enough to refuel and allow Bush to call the White House. He learned that three men besides the president had been wounded: a Secret Service agent; a Washington, D.C., police officer; and Jim Brady, the White House press secretary. The president was already in surgery at George Washington University Hospital and there was no word yet on his condition.

The meaning of the phrase "no more than a heartbeat from the presidency" must have come home to Bush on March 30, 1981, when he learned that President Ronald Reagan had been shot. He is shown here arriving at the White House to meet with the cabinet and the National Security Council.

As he reboarded *Air Force Two*, Bush could not help but think about the assassination of President John F. Kennedy in 1963 and how quickly Lyndon Johnson, then vice president, had to take charge and immediately begin making critical decisions. Bush didn't know what to expect upon his return to Washington. Reporters traveling with the vice president, and sitting in another part of the plane, were frustrated. They heard what had happened, but had even less information than Bush. Finally, the call came in about an hour before *Air Force Two* landed in Washington; the president was out of surgery and out of danger.

Bush still had work to do. As soon as he could get to the White House, he called a meeting with the president's cabinet and the National Security Council, which advises the president on foreign affairs.

Under the 25th Amendment to the U.S. Constitution, if the president is unable to carry out his duties, the vice president can immediately assume the powers and duties of Acting President. But Bush only got to be "acting" president for a short period. President Reagan recovered quickly from his gunshot wound.

Special Assignments • During his vice presidency, Bush was given several special assignments by President Reagan. Early in their first term of office, Reagan was able to follow through on one of his campaign promises—to reduce the number of federal government regulations that made business, and people's lives in general, so complicated.

Bush was named chairman of a special Task Force on Regulatory Relief to study ways to fulfill that

During Ronald Reagan's second term, Bush participated in such vice-presidential functions as the annual White House Easter egg roll. He is shown here with his wife Barbara and the Easter bunny.

In the fall of 1985, in Moscow at the funeral of General Secretary M. Andropov, Bush met the new Soviet leader (left) General Secretary Mikhail Gorbachev.

promise. The result was a report that made several recommendations to eliminate or change unnecessary federal rules and regulations, many of which were adopted.

The South Florida Task Force, formed by Bush in 1982, was less successful. Created in response to an appeal by citizens in Miami to help curb drug traffic in the area, the task force is given credit for bringing together several federal government agencies to fight international drug smuggling. But cocaine imports actually increased while the task force was in operation and marijuana dealers simply moved their operations to other areas.

The U.S. Task Force on Combatting Terrorism, which Bush also headed, produced a politically popular recommendation—that the United States government make no agreements with terrorists, who were hijacking planes and blowing up cars and buildings, often killing innocent people.

But that suggestion was thrown out when the United States attempted to secretly trade weapons with Iran for the release of American hostages.

Bush for President • By the end of 1984, when he was about to begin his second term as vice president, Bush had all but made up his mind to run for president in 1988.

Standing on a boat confiscated from drug smugglers, Vice President Bush looks over at bales of marijuana in another boat as containers of cocaine were placed on a cooler in front of him for inspection. Bush's antidrug campaign had little effect in stopping drug smuggling into the United States.

In the 1984 presidential campaign, Vice President Bush debated Democratic vice-presidential candidate Geraldine Ferraro. Later, his locker room language in summing up the debate angered many feminists.

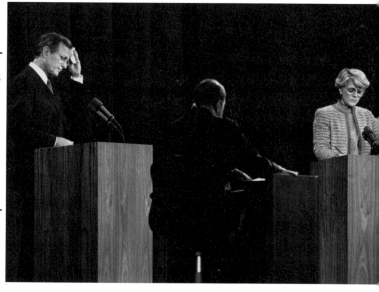

Barbara and George Bush at Kennebunkport,
surrounded by their children and spouses,
and their grandchildren

He wasted little time getting organized, bringing together some of the same people who had helped get Ronald Reagan elected. The early start turned out to be a smart move. As the campaign began to heat up and his success was clear, Bush could attribute it to his organization, good long-range planning, and a strong staff. But he didn't get through the campaign without some criticism. People began to question his leadership abilities. The press began to look into his role in the Iran-Contra affair, in which the United States had secretly sold weapons to Iran and then diverted the profits to Nicaraguan Contras, a rebel group trying to overthrow the government. And unlike eight years earlier, he wouldn't be able to take full advantage of Ronald Reagan's popularity. This was Bush's campaign; it was his turn to be the leader.

★ Six ★
PRESIDENT BUSH

The presidential campaign began to come into focus following the Democratic and Republican parties' national conventions. First, the Democrats chose Massachusetts Governor Michael Dukakis as their candidate. As his running mate, Dukakis picked Lloyd Bentsen, the Texas senator who had beaten Bush in their Senate race almost twenty years earlier.

In accepting the Republican presidential nomination, Bush pledged that, if elected president, he would never raise taxes and would create 30 million jobs. Bush's nomination as his party's candidate was hardly news, but his selection of a running mate caught just about everyone by surprise, including some of Bush's own aides and President Reagan. Bush's selection of Dan Quayle, a forty-one-year-old

*George Bush and Senator Dan Quayle raise
their arms together after Bush named Quayle as
his running mate at the Republican convention.*

senator from Indiana, to run with him as the vice
presidential candidate appeared to be a mistake from
the moment he was picked.

Quayle, everyone soon learned, had used his
wealthy family's influence to join the National Guard
rather than risk being drafted for combat duty in Viet-

nam. By joining the National Guard, Quayle did nothing illegal. But his Guard duty didn't look good to many voters, especially since, as a U.S. senator, he had been a strong supporter of the military. Bush aides, concerned that Quayle would damage the campaign, urged Bush to "dump" Quayle in favor of a stronger, perhaps better known, running mate. But Bush decided to keep Dan Quayle on the presidential ticket, and eventually other issues, more to Bush's favor, came to dominate the news.

For one thing, Bush favored the death penalty; Michael Dukakis was against it. Bush believed that school children should be required to say the Pledge of Allegiance; Dukakis, a lawyer, pointed out that the U.S. Supreme Court had already ruled that requiring the pledge to be said in school was unconstitutional. Thus, Dukakis couldn't support this requirement; Bush had implied that Dukakis was unpatriotic.

Bush also called Dukakis weak on crime. Throughout much of the campaign, Bush television commercials noted the case of Willie Horton, a black murder convict who attacked a woman and her companion while on a weekend furlough from a Massachusetts prison. Many states and the federal government give prisoners furloughs, and the Massachusetts furlough program had actually been put

Top left: Bush campaigning in Massachusetts, home state of Governor Michael Dukakis. Here he is with Boston policemen. The headline reads, "Boston Police Endorse Bush." Top right: Projecting the image of a healthy candidate, Bush was often photographed jogging or participating in other sports. Left: Like almost every other politician, Bush kissed his share of babies on the campaign trail.

*George Bush raises his right hand as he is sworn
into office as the forty-first president of the
United States. Chief Justice William Rehnquist
administers the oath of office, and First Lady
Barbara Bush holds the Bible for her husband.*

into effect under a former Republican governor, but the Bush TV commercials declared that "Dukakis not only opposes the death penalty, he allowed first-degree murderers to have weekend passes from prison." Dukakis eventually answered Bush's attack, but his answers came too late to have the same impact as the commercials. Dukakis supporters charged that the Bush commercials stirred up racism.

Drugs were another major campaign issue; Bush said he would name Dan Quayle to head his war on drugs. Bush also supported increased business development efforts for blacks and other minorities by the federal government. And he promised to expand the National Park system.

As the campaign progressed, both Bush and Dukakis, at the urging of their advisors, talked less and less to reporters covering the campaign. Many questions on issues that were important in helping people decide how to vote didn't get answered. As a result, nearly half of the nation's eligible voters didn't vote, primarily, they said, according to polls because they didn't like the way both candidates handled themselves during the campaign.

On November 8, 1988, George Herbert Walker Bush was elected the forty-first President of the United States with 54 percent of the popular vote, while winning forty states with 426 electoral votes. Dukakis won 46 percent—ten states and the District of Columbia, for 112 electoral votes. After nearly a quarter-century in public life, starting out his political career on a Republican party committee in a largely Democratic area of suburban Fort Worth, Texas, George Bush had made it to the top.

★ Index ★

Anderson, John, 38, 40
Assassination attempt, 1981, 46–50

Baker, Howard H., Jr., 37, 38
Benton, William, 8
Bentsen, Lloyd, 56
Brady, Jim, 48
Breen, Jon, 38
Bruce, David, 31
Bush, Barbara Pierce, 13, 14–16
Bush, Dorothy, 19
Bush, Dorothy Walker, 7, 8, 9
Bush, George Herbert Walker:
    Ambassador to UN, 23–25
    birth, 7
    Chief of liaison to China, 31–32
    childhood, 8–10
    Director of the CIA, 32–35
    early political career, 19–22
    education, 10, 16
    marriage, 14
    Presidential campaign, 1978–80, 36–42
    Presidential campaign, 1984–88, 52–62
    Republican National Committee, 27–30
    Texas oilman, 17–19
    Vice President, 43–52
    World War II, 10–14
Bush, George, Jr., 19
Bush, Jeb, 19
Bush, Jonathon, 9
Bush, Marvin, 19
Bush, Nancy, 9
Bush, Neil, 19
Bush, Prescott Sheldon, 7–8
Bush, Prescott Sheldon, Jr., 7, 9

Bush, Robin, 18–19

Carter, Jimmy, 35, 36, 42, 43, 45
Colby, William, 34
Crane, Phil, 38

Delaney, Jack, 13, 14
Dole, Robert, 27, 38
Dukakis, Michael, 56, 58–62

Ford, Gerald R., 30–31, 32, 42

Greenwich Country Day School,
   10

Haig, Alexander, 48
Horton, Willie, 58

Iran-contra affair, 52, 55

Johnson, Lyndon, 49

Kennebunkport, Maine, 8
Kennedy, John F., 49
Kissinger, Henry, 32

Mallon, Neil, 17

Mao Tse-tung, 32
Mondale, Walter, 43

Nadeau, Leo, 13
Nixon, Richard, 23, 25–26, 27, 30

Phillips Academy, 10

Quayle, Dan, 56–58, 61

Reagan, Ronald, 37–40, 42, 43,
   45, 46, 55, 56
Rockefeller, Nelson A., 31
Rogers, Kenny, 42

Schultz, George, 26–27
Smith College, 16
Stimson, Henry, 10

Walker, David, 8
Walker, George Herbert, 8
Walker, Herbert, 17
Walker, John, 18–19
Watergate scandal, 29–30
White, William G., 13, 14

Yale University, 16